Neem: Benefits for Health and the Environment

By

Pamela Paterson

Published by Writer Types Inc.

ISBN-13: 978-1470001438

Design by Rhys Griffiths

Cover design by NATWORK, www.natwork.ca

Edited by Robert Long

Contents

Contents

Contents

Preface

Neem is a marvelous ancient plant with bountiful benefits for health and the environment. Even the greatest skeptics acknowledge how marvelous neem can be. This book explores the benefits of neem for health and the environment based on the scientific literature available.

Note to Reader

The information and advice provided in this book are not intended as a substitution for the advice of your physician or healthcare professionals. Consult your physician and healthcare professionals for all issues that may require medical attention or diagnosis, including before administering or undertaking any course of treatment or diet. Neither the author nor the publisher shall be liable or responsible for any loss or damage allegedly arising from any information or suggestion in this book, nor for websites or their content that are referred to in this book.

A Word from Dr. Bruce Jarvis

Neem is renowned as a marvelous ancient plant, according to Dr. Bruce Jarvis, Professor Emeritus, Department of Chemistry and Biochemistry, University of Maryland:

> Much of modern pharmacopeia as well as our agricultural resources can be traced back to indigenous plants that our ancestors first made use of thousands of years ago.
>
> Neem is a quintessential example of such a plant that even today has much to tell us about how nature works and how, with thoughtful scientific investigation, our lives can continue to be enriched by this marvelous ancient plant.
>
> This book presents many of the fascinating details about this wonderful plant that you will find well worth reading.

Acknowledgements

I would like to gratefully acknowledge the support of two key people in the development of this book.

Dr. Bruce Jarvis: for all of his valued assistance with the scientific paper which was the basis of this book. Only an email away, Dr. Jarvis provided immediate and thoughtful comments that assisted me in formulating my topic and working through my myriad of queries. He epitomizes dedication to the teaching of science.

Robert Long: for his detailed eye and passion for creating quality content. A trusted editor and friend, he uses the finest combination of work ethic and intellect to arrive at wonderful results.

About Neem

1

The neem tree (*Azadirachta indica*) and its chemical products have been used for centuries in many facets for human utility—as food, wood, a heating source, a pesticide, a soil amendment, an agrochemical, and a significant healing agent for purportedly over 100 diseases (Neem Foundation). It is incredibly diverse in its geography, natural habitat, and reproductive biology.

This book provides a technical discussion of neem based on scientific literature. For information about how you can use neem day–to–day for your health, refer to www.abaconeem.com.

Getting to Know Neem

Neem is truly a tree with roots firmly embedded in the cultures of its people. For 2,000 years in India neem twigs have been chewed on to clean teeth, neem leaf juice applied on skin to treat disorders, neem tea drunken as a tonic, and neem leaves placed in the home to ward away bugs (Muñoz–Valenzuela 2007).

Its fruit (about the size of an olive) are eaten raw or cooked, and young twigs and flowers are sometimes eaten as vegetables. The fruit is also a major food source for birds and bats (they eat the pulp, not the seed), among others. The gum (resin), which is colorless, sticky, and malodorous, is also a high–protein food additive used in Southeast Asia, known as "neem glue". Even the leaves are a source of food—they are used as fodder in the dry season (AgroForestryTree Database).

Neem also has important fuel uses: the wood is used as firewood and to produce excellent–grade charcoal, and the oil is used as lamp oil throughout India. The timber, although it has a rough grain and does not polish well, is used locally to make furniture. Its popularity in being used to make furniture is partly due to its insect repellent properties, for insects are deterred from coming near the furniture or the items inside. The wood is also popular for fencing and construction. In addition, the tree bark has 12% to 14% tannins, which makes it a good source for tannin chemicals (AgroForestryTree Database).

Neem has a well–developed root system that can extract nutrients from lower soil levels, making it an important agent in erosion control because it is virtually drought–resistant. As such it is useful as a dune fixation tree. Farmers in India use neem cake (the residue left after extracting oil from the seeds) as an organic manure and soil amendment; it enhances the efficiency of nitrogen fertilizers by reducing the rate of nitrification and hampering pests such as nematodes, fungi, and insects (AgroForestryTree Database).

Geography and Habitat

Neem has extensive geographic distribution which contributes to significant variation in its botanical description.

Geographic Distribution

The neem tree is native to India, Indonesia, Malaysia, Myanmar, Pakistan, Senegal, Sri Lanka, and Thailand. It has since been transplanted to many parts of the world, including several countries in Africa, South America, Latin America, the Caribbean, Bahamas, Middle East, and others (AgroForestryTree Database). In the United States, neem is grown in Florida and California.

Botanical Description

The neem tree (*Azadirachta indica*), a member of the Meliaceae family (Mahogany family), is also called the Indian neem tree, Indian lilac, and Margosa tree (Barceloux 2008).

Neem populations are heterogeneous in all respects, owing greatly to differences in soil and climate. The trees themselves are known to have genetic variation in height, bark, size and taste of fruit, branching type, leaf form, and color (Muñoz–Valenzuela 2007).

Height generally ranges from 15 to 25 m, or even 30 m with limbs of 15 m in length. Neem has a large, round crown of about 10 m (maximum 20 m) in diameter. These foliage proportions provide for shade nearly year–round (AgroForestryTree Database; Cseke, et al. 2006; Barceloux 2008).

Figure 1-1: Neem tree

Shiny dark green leaves are pinnately compound (leaflets attached in two rows to the main vein). The 10 to 12 serrated leaflets on each leaf are 7 cm long by 2.5 cm wide and the leaf blade is glabrous (Barceloux 2008; Muñoz–Valenzuela 2007). When damaged, the leaves emit a garlic odor.

White flowers are found as inflorescences with joined sepals.

Figure 1-2: Neem flowers

As shown in Figure 1-3, the fruit is yellow, fleshy, and resembles an olive. It is about 1 to 2 cm long and has one, or infrequently, two seeds (Barceloux 2008).

Like other characteristics of the tree population, the fruit form, size, weight, kernel proportion, composition, and oil content and quality are also varied (Muñoz–Valenzuela 2007).

Figure 1-3: Neem fruit and leaves

Natural Habitat

Except for waterlogged soil, neem can grow in almost any climate in the lowland tropics, ranging from mixed forest in India, lowland monsoon forest in Indonesia, evergreen forest and dry deciduous forest in Africa (AgroForestryTree Database), to more recently the Caribbean, Bahamas, California, and Florida.

Neem can grow within an altitude range of 0 to 1500 m, and tolerate conditions to 40°C with a mean annual rainfall of 400 to 1200 mm (AgroForestryTree Database).

The adult neem is able to tolerate some frost, but requires a significant amount of sunlight. The young neem, on the other hand, can grow at least for the first few years in areas that are predominantly shaded, but is not able to tolerate frost (AgroForestryTree Database).

Neem can grow in soils from neutral to alkaline, but the optimum pH is 6.2 to 7. It can also live well on shallow, stony, sandy soils, or where there is a hard calcareous or clay pan near the surface (AgroForestryTree Database). In an ideal habitat, neem can live 150 to 200 years (Neem Foundation).

Reproductive Biology

Neem first produces white fragrant blossoms, then develops hard green fruits which are bitter to the taste. Subsequently, the flesh (pericarp) softens and the fruit changes color to yellow. The ripe yellow fruit is sweet. From the beginning of the flowering stage to the seed falling (after the fruit shrivels away), is 27 weeks (Cseke, et al. 2006; Johnson et al. 1996).

At four or five years old, neem can produce flowers and fruit, but only after 10 to 12 years will it produce economically viable seed quantities (AgroForestryTree Database). A mature tree produces 30 to 50 kg fruit annually (Neem Foundation), or even as much as 50 to 100 kg of fruit per year (Cseke, et al. 2006). It is pollinated by insects such as honey bees. Neem may be self–incompatible, as some isolated trees do not set fruit (AgroForestryTree Database).

The flowering and fruiting seasons vary, depending on the region and time of year. For example, in Thailand neem produces flowers and fruits year–round whereas in East Africa, with its defined dry and wet seasons, it does not (AgroForestryTree Database).

Chemical Compounds

2

Chemically, neem is very rich and complex. It has pharmacologically useful compounds in every part of the tree, and these are extracted through traditional and commercial means. By far, the most renowned chemical is azadirachtin, which is specific to the neem tree.

Chemically Rich Neem

Neem is chemically rich. There are over 300 plant secondary compounds. Most of the active compounds are terpenoids, found in the fruit, seeds, twigs, stem, and root bark. Of most prominence and of most commercial use is the tetranortripernoid azadirachtin (a liminoid) in the seed kernels, the main ingredient in many commercial products, including insecticides (Koul, et al. 2004).

Extraction and Formulation

Indian farmers are known to grind the kernels or leaves and use water to extract the chemicals, and then spray this suspension over plants (Cseke, et al. 2006).

For commercial–scale extraction and concentration of azadirachtin, ethanol is most often used as the solvent because limonoids are very soluble in alcohols. The seeds are crushed and then soaked in alcohol either at that time or after extracting the oil component with hexane. These aqueous extracts can then be applied directly to the crop either with or without a wetting agent. If needing to be stored for a long term or transported a far distance, azadirachtin can be extracted and sold as a concentrate. Some additives such as the antioxidants sesame oil or paraaminobenzoic acid (natural pesticides from Chrysanthemum spp.) protect the liminoids from ultraviolet damage (Cseke, et al. 2006).

Neem Oil Composition

Neem oil extract, which is the fatty acid extract of neem tree seeds, is the most widely used product of the neem tree. Neem oil is yellowish in color, malodorous, and has an unpleasant taste due to the sulfur compounds (Barceloux 2008). Neem seeds are about 45% oil (AgroForestryTree Database), and provide the major source of neem chemicals. Should a neem tree produce 50 to 100 kg of fruit it can yield approximately 10 kg of neem oil per year (Cseke, et al. 2006).

Neem oil primarily consists of glycerides of oleic and stearic acids, at 50% and 20%, respectively (Gokhale, et al. 2009). Neem oil also contains at least 35 pharmacologically active compounds and a number of other compounds such as flavonoids and sulfur compounds, at varying concentrations (Cseke, et al. 2006; Barceloux 2008).

Of these pharmacologically active compounds, the azadirachtins are the most bioactive and popular commercially. In addition to the azadirachtins, the other major liminoids are the salannins and nimbins. Compounds from these groups comprise at least 80% of the neem seed extract by weight (Isman, 1997).

Chemistry of Azadirachtin

Azadirachtin, found only in *Azadirachta sp.* (Capinera 2008), is a complex tetranortriterpenoid liminoid from the neem seed. Neem seeds have 4 to 6 g/ kg of azadirachtin, depending on the ecotype of the tree and local conditions (Mordue (Luntz) et al. 2000).

Analogues

Of all of the liminoids in neem, azadirachtin and its about 25 natural analogues are the most biologically active (Devakumar and Kumar 2008). Of these, azadirachtin-A (Aza A) is the most plentiful and biologically active, and the one that is used most for commercial insecticides (Barceloux 2008; (Cseke, et al. 2006). Aza A is about 80% of the azadirachtin found in neem, while up to 15% of the azadirachtin may be Aza B (3-tigloylazadirachtol) (Devakumar and Kumar 2008).

Azadirachtin A   Azadirachtin B

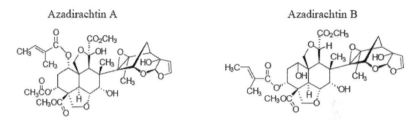

Figure 2-1: Azadirachtin A C35H44O16 and Azadirachtin B, C33H42O14 (Newfoundland Forestry Service, 2002)

Properties

Of the triterpenoids isolated from neem, azadirachtin is the most oxygenated, and one of the most polar (Johnson et al. 1996). It has 16 stereogenic centers, 7 of which are quaternary. The water solubility is negligible, at 50 ug/mL, which has been a limiting factor in its use as a biopesticide or in herbal medicine in natural form (Liu et al. 2005).

Because azadirachtin has acid and base sensitive functional groups, it tends toward instability in acids and bases, and this consideration must be taken into account when choosing a suitable solvent and developing formulations. Another factor in its instability is that azadirachtin is UV–labile due to its many double bonds (Free Patents Online).

Liminoids have as a precursor the 4,4,8-trimethyl-17-furanyl steroid skeleton, and through oxidative degradation four carbons are lost from the side chain. Azadirachtin is believed to be biosynthesized from the steroid precursor tirucallol (Dewick 2001).

Synthesis

While azadirachtin was first isolated in 1968, its structure was not determined conclusively until 1987 (Ishaaya, et al. 2007). Its synthesis in the laboratory would elude scientists for 20 subsequent years. Until that point, the two subfragments decalin and hydroxy furan were synthesized. Interestingly, each of these subfragments had their own insecticidal effects (Collinge, et al. 2008).

In 2007, Steve Ley and colleagues (40 PhD students over 20 years) finally synthesized azadirachtin in a process involving a Claisen rearrangement for the formation of a C8-C14 bond and radical cyclization to form the bridged ring system. In the synthesis, decalin was derived from azadirachtin in its natural form (Veitch, 2007; Devakumar and Kumar, 2008). This 20–year effort illustrates the true complexity of azadirachtin.

Insecticide & Pesticide   3

Neem has impressive and far–reaching pesticide properties, most notably as an insecticide. It targets insects in a number of effective ways while causing no harm to humans—truly impressive when compared to synthetic pesticides.

Insecticide

By far, the most widespread use of neem has been as an insecticide. Azadirachtin is the predominant biologically active chemical in most insect–based bioassays, and is known as the "most potent insect antifeedant discovered to date" (Ishaaya, et al. 2007). These antifeedant effects were first discovered in 1952 by Heinrich Schmutterer who found that desert locusts (*Schistocerca gregaria,* Forscal) did not eat the neem tree (Koul, et al. 2004). *S. gregaria* had a very high sensitivity to azadirachtin, postulated because of co–evolutionary origins of the neem tree and locust to Burma (Mordue (Luntz) et al. 2000).

Broad Range as Insecticide

Scientific research indicates azadirachtin is active in nearly 550 insect species (Anuradha and Annadurai, 2008), showing it to be a potent insecticide in the following orders (AgroForestryTree Database):

- Coleoptera—beetles and weevils
- Dictyoptera—cockroaches and mantids
- Diptera— flies
- Heteroptera— true bugs
- Homoptera—aphids, leaf hoppers, wasps, and ants
- Isoptera—termites
- Lepidoptera—moths and butterflies
- Orthoptera—grasshoppers, katydids
- Siphonaptera—fleas
- Thysanoptera—thrips.

Important! Although azadirachtin is active in these species, this does not mean the presence of a neem tree will eradicate all insects in its vicinity. Azadirarchtin must be formally extracted from the neem seed. In fact, Abaco Neem, an organic neem farm in the Bahamas, reports that insects— particularly beneficial insects—flourish on their farm.

Few Serious Enemies

Neem possesses potency towards insects, while having few serious pests of its own. Exceptions include scale insect *Aonidiella orientalis* and the tea mosquito bug *Helopeltis antonii.* There are over 35 known pests that feed on the neem tree sap, bark, roots, shoots, and leaves. These pests include shoot borers, Microtermes, fungus (*Psuedocercospora subsesessilis*), mistletoes (*Dendrophtoe falcate, Tapinanthus spp*), and bacteria (*Pseudomonas azadirachtae*) (AgroForestryTree Database; Cseke, et al. 2006).

Effects and Mode of Action on Insects

Insects in which azadirachtin is bioactive may be affected in a variety of ways.

Azadirachtin may act as an antifeedancy, causing the insect to perish by anorexia. In addition, it may interfere with insect growth regulation, causing reduced and abnormal growth as well as increased mortality. Furthermore, azadirachtin may cause reproductive and sterility problems, interfere with proper cellular processes and cell synthetic machinery, and affect muscles.

Table 3-1 illustrates how azadirachtin affects insects as well as the mode of action in which the target is affected (Anuradha and Annadurai 2008; Mordue (Luntz) et al. 2000; Koul, et al. 2004).

Table 3-1: Summary of Azadirachtin Effects on Insects

Effects / Target	Mode of Action
Primary antifeedancy Target: Mouthpart & other chemoreceptors Azadirachtin activates deterrent cells in chemoreceptors	Azadirachtin activates deterrent cells in chemoreceptors, interferes with other chemoreceptors for taste perception, and blocks firing of "sugar" receptor cells that are integral in stimulating feeding. These combined effects result in death by anorexia.
Secondary antifeedancy Target: Gut	Azadirachtin inhibits peristalsis, reduces enzyme production as food moves through gut, inhibits midgut cell replacement, and reduces feeding.

Table 3-1: Summary of Azadirachtin Effects on Insects

Effects / Target	Mode of Action
Insect growth regulation

Target: Cuticle | Azadirachtin as an ecdysone agonist causes alterations to ecdysteroid and Juvenile Hormone (JH) titers by blocking the release of morphogenetic peptides from the brain, causing reduced growth, increased mortality, and abnormal and delayed molts. |
| Sterility / Reproduction

Target: Reproductive organs | Azadirachtin disrupts the JH titers and ovarian ecdysteroid production, leading to a reduction in the number of viable eggs and live progeny.

Azadirachtin affects the formation of spermatozoa.
In desert locus *S. gregaria* testes, there was "major cytogenetic effects" on spermatogenesis when injected in the 5th instar.

In a dose–dependent manner, the binding of azadirachtin to *S. gregaria* sperm tails is essentially irreversible. More specifically, azadirachtin binds to the axoneme (cell cytoskeletal element) of the tails of developing sperm in the testes follicles. |
| Cellular processes

Target: Dividing cells | Azadirachtin blocks cell division in meiosis and mitosis.

For example, in the Mexican bean beetle, *Epilachna varivestis*, azadirachtin caused "massive tissue degeneration" where there should be active cell division, such as in the wing discs of developing larvae, the fat body, ovary, and testes.

In the fruit fly *Drosophila melanogaster* (Dipteran), the primary target of azadirachtin *in vivo* and *in silico* is actin, which is down–regulated. Azadirachtin adversely affects rapidly dividing cells and causes cell cycle arrest by not allowing the correct microtubule orientation during spindle assembly in the axonemes. |

Table 3-1: Summary of Azadirachtin Effects on Insects

Effects / Target	Mode of Action
Target: Muscles	Azadirachtin causes a loss of muscle tone.
Target: Cell synthetic machinery	Azadirachtin blocks digestive enzyme production in the gut, and inhibits protein synthesis in various tissues. Protein synthesis inhibition also reduces the levels of detoxification enzymes in insects, thus possibly having a useful role in reducing insect resistance.

Variation in Efficacy

With respect to Table 3-1, azadirachtin caused toxic insect growth regulatory (IGR) effects in all species tested, but with antifeedancy there was a tremendous amount of variation depending on insect order and species in the orders (Mordue (Luntz) et al. 2000). In fact, some species are "behaviorally indifferent" to azadirachtin (Ishaaya, et al. 2007).

Such is the case with *Melanoplus sanguinipes* (Fab.), otherwise known as the North American Plains grasshopper. *M. sanguinipes* has no co–evolutionary pattern with neem and therefore has no chemoreceptors that respond negatively to it (Mordue (Luntz) et al. 2000).

On the other hand, the desert locust *S. gregaria* within the same order of Orthoptera is very sensitive to azadirachtin and will not feed on it (Mordue (Luntz) et al. 2000).

The range of sensitivities per orders is shown in Table 3-2, from the highly sensitive Lepidoptera to the less sensitive orders.

Table 3-2: Sensitivity of Insects to Azadirachtin

Order	ED_{50} (ppm)
Lepidoptera	< 0.001 – 50
Coleoptera	100 – 500
Hemiptera	100 – 500
Hymenoptera	100 – 500
Orthoptera	0.001 – > 1000

Not only does the efficacy of neem vary among orders, but even among species within the same order (Mordue (Luntz) et al. 2000). When the concentrated azadirachtin product NeemAzal®–T/S was tested for larvicidal activity on three mosquito species, the LC50 results varied tremendously as follows: *Anopheles stephensi* (1.92 ppm), *Aedes aegypti* (8.42 ppm), and *Culex quinquefasciatus* (15.87 ppm) (Gunasekaran, et al. 2003).

Effects on Beneficial Pests

Neem has little if any effect on beneficial pests, such as spiders, lady beetles, parasitic wasps, and predatory mites, nor does it affect levels of honey bee pollinations or worker bees (Hall and Menn 1999).

Only in rare instances is it reported in scientific literature that neem has had negative effects on non-target species. For example, in the case of *Harmonia axyridis* Pallas, a beetle which feeds on the North American soybean aphid *Aphis glycines* Matsumura, neem formulations containing azadirachtin reduced *H. axyridis* instar survival to adulthood, as well as delayed development (Kraiss and Cullen 2008).

In addition, the University of Delaware reported high levels of toxicity for fish exposed to azadirachtin, as shown in Table 3-3. There were negligible levels of toxicity for bees and none for birds.

Table 3-3: Toxicity of Azadirachtin Insecticidal Products (University of Delaware)

Name	LD_{50} Values Mg/Kg		Toxicity		
	Oral	Dermal	Bird	Fish	Bee
Azadirachtin, Aza–Direct, Azatin, Ecozin, Neemix	>5,000	>2,000	--	H	N
Aza-Direct, azadirachtin	>5,000	>2,000	--	H	N
Azatin, azadirachtin	>5,000	>2,000	--	H	N

In summary, despite some instances of toxicity, the U.S. Environmental Protection Agency (EPA) recognizes the overall safety of neem. The EPA has indicated through its product labelling categories that the oral LD_{50} values of neem are so low that out of the four toxicity categories for severities of product labelling (danger, warning, caution, and none), it is the least toxic toward humans and does not require any signal word in labelling at all. Dermal LD_{50} values are also low, but do require a label of caution (University of Delaware, EPA).

Pesticide Potential

While neem is most well–known as an insecticide, it has also shown promise as a pesticide for controlling rodents, pathogens, and fish bacteria.

Neem has been suggested as an effective infertility agent in controlling populations of rodents, such as rats (Morovati et al. 2008).

It has also been shown to be effective in controlling foodborne pathogens, making it a potential agent against food spoilage bacteria (Hoque et al. 2007).

Neem even has a potential application in the fisheries industry, having been cited as effective against the pathogen *Aeromonas hydrophila* in goldfish, which causes ulcerative dermatitis and "significant losses to fisheries and fish culture" (Harikrishnan and Balasundaram, 2008).

Pesticidal Formulations

With respect to the "best" formulation of neem chemicals for a pesticide, there is no "magic bullet" but in fact several factors that contribute to effective formulations.

Combination Formulations

Interestingly, the natural proportions of chemicals in neem are generally known to be more effective than azadirachtin alone, and in many cases, azadirachtin used in combination with other herbal compounds provides even better efficacy. Adding other neem liminoids such as nimbandiol, deacetylsalannin, deacetylnimbin, nimbin, and 6-acetylnimbandiol to azadirachtin insecticides have been shown to improve efficacy (Hall and Menn 1999).

For example, as a molluscide, the combination of *Lawsonia inermis* seed powder (Henna), cedar oil (*Cedrus deodara* Roxh), and neem oil (*Azadirachta indica A.* Juss) was more toxic than individual applications of those and several other natural products against *Lymnaea acuminate* and *Indoplanorbis exustus* (snails) (Singh and Singh 2001).

And, when neem oil cakes and karanja (*Pongamia glabra*) oil cake were used in combination against three mosquito species (*Culex quinquefasciatus* (say), *Aedes aegypti* (L.) and *Anopheles stephensi* (L.)), the efficacy increased from 4 to 10 fold for the LC50, and 2 to 6 fold for the LC95 over individual applications (Shanmugasundaram, et al. 2008).

Natural Instability

The natural instability of azadirachtin (refer to "Chemistry of Azadirachtin" on page 14) that causes it to need frequent reapplication as an insecticide, may be solved by synthesizing stable derivatives of azadirachtin, as was shown with tetrahydroazadirachtin-A (THA) when it was sprayed on okra crops *Abelmoschus esculentus* (L.) Moench. for the whitefly (*Bemisia tabaci* (Genn.)) and leaf hopper (jassid) *Amrasca biguttulla* (Ishida) (Dhingra, S., et al. 2008).

Use of Adjuvants

It has also been suggested that the use of adjuvants would increase the effectiveness of neem–based insecticides. Although azadirachtin will move across the leaf cuticle, it has limited motility from leaf to leaf—adjuvants increase the motility. As with the formulations of neem products, results among adjuvants vary. Against first instar nymphs *Trialeurodes vaporariorum* (greenhouse whitefly) on tomato, Neemix® solutions in combination with adjuvants that contained vegetable or mineral oil (Joint Venture® and Soydex®) facilitated the highest mortality. The mortality for Neemix® alone was 33%, Neemix®–Soydex® was 92%, and Neemix®–Joint Venture® was 91% (Hall and Menn 1999).

Use as a Commercial Insecticide

Currently, many commercial insecticides are being marketed worldwide. For example, Neemix® has been used in the U.S. for food crops since 1993 (Hall and Menn, 1999). Neemix® and another insecticide Bioneem® have been found to be comparable in efficacy to organophosphate pesticides (Watson and Preedy 2008).

Advantages and Disadvantages

Considering that organic synthetic insecticides are more dangerous, leave toxic residues in food, are not readily biodegradable (Peshin and Dhawan 2009), and can harm beneficial pests, neem offers a sound alternative in these respects.

While neem is not as powerful as synthetic agents such as permethrin and DEET (Vatandoost and Hanafi–Bojd 2008), the fact that neem is generally recognized as safe provides a compelling reason to consider neem as part of an integrated approach against pests.

Future Outlook as an Insecticide

Neem by most accounts offers a promising future against pests, including as a mosquito repellent. It can be a "very component of an integrated approach against malaria transmission because of its efficacy, local availability, low cost, and safety, especially when compared to synthetic insecticides (Gianotti, et al. 2008).

Since neem does not kill adult insects, neem–based insecticides tend to be used with other strategies like adulticides or beneficial pests (Hall and Menn 1999). As part of an integrated approach against pests, neem offers a respectable alternative and its future is promising.

Human Medicine

4

Traditionally, Neem has been used as a medicinal agent for more than 2,000 years to treat more than 100 diseases (Neem Foundation). In Western medicine, neem also has several strong promoters in the medical community, including many prominent physicians such as television host Dr. Mehmet Oz.

While this track record is impressive, in keeping with the research–based approach of this book, published scientific studies rather than anecdotal evidence has been surveyed in assessing the medicinal applications of neem.

For a broader discussion of the health benefits of neem and how you can use it to treat your ailments, refer to www.abaconeem.com.

Medicinal Applications

In traditional medicine, all parts of the neem tree are used—flowers, seeds, fruits, roots, bark, and in particular, leaves to treat more than 100 diseases (Subapriya et al. 2005; Neem Foundation).

In Western medicine, primarily the seeds, leaves, and bark have been studied. They have shown impressive medicinal properties and in fact, the list of reported medicinal benefits in published studies is extensive, as shown in Table 4-1 (AgroForestryTree Database; Cseke, et al. 2006; Subapriya et al. 2005; Boeke et al. 2004; Talwar et al. 1997; Liu et al. 2005).

Table 4-1: Medicinal Applications of Neem

• Abortifacient	• Antimalarial	• Antiulcer
• Anti–implantation	• Antiseptic	• Antiviral
• Anti–inflammatory	• Antirheumatic	• Antiworm
• Antibacterial	• Antimicrobial	• Boils
• Anticarcinogenic	• Antimutagenic	• Blood detoxifier
• Anticlotting	• Antioxidant	• Diuretic
• Antifertility	• Antiparasitic	• Eye diseases
• Antifungal	• Antiperiodic	• Immunomodulatory
• Antihepatic	• Antiperiodontic	• Pimples
• Antihyperglycemic	• Antipurgative	• Skin diseases
• Antileprosy	• Antituberculosis	• Spermicidal

In the information that follows, select medicinal applications are discussed in more detail.

Cancer

A number of neem chemicals have been shown to be active in several cancer studies, including prostate, colon, and breast.

Neem extract induces apoptosis of prostate cancer cells (PC-3) (Kumar et al. 2006). The triterpenoid nimbolide showed antigrowth activity of moderate to very strong in human colon carcinoma HT-29 cells (Roy et al. 2006).

Another neem tetranortriterpenoid, gedunin, possesses anticancer properties as an Hsp90 (heat shock protein 90) inhibitor. Hsp90 is becoming a leading therapeutic target of interest in cancer research. It is known as a chaperone protein, and the proteins chaperoned by Hsp90 are called client proteins. The protein–folding machinery of Hsp90 is responsible for folding client proteins into their biologically active form. When mutations or abnormal expression of these client proteins occur, cancer may result. As Hsp90 maintains the function of these cancer promoting, or oncogenic, client proteins, it is a worthy target to inhibit because it results in apoptosis in the cells of these client proteins. The proteins are degraded and tumor progression is inhibited. Gedunin does not bind competitively versus ATP, but its exact mechanism of action is unknown. The natural gedunin, as opposed to the 19 semisynthetic derivatives of gedunin, performed the best (Brandt et al. 2008; Infinity Pharmaceuticals).

A neem leaf preparation (NLP) was also shown to induce apoptosis in tumor cells—not directly, but through stimulating human peripheral blood mononuclear cells (PBMC), which in turn caused antiproliferative activity in tumor cells as well as induced apoptosis via the release of cytotoxic cytokines (Bose et al. 2007).

In mice and rats, NLP was shown to enhance the breast tumor associated antigen (BTAA). The antibodies produced by BTAA-NLP immunization induced cytotoxicity in MCF-7 cells (human breast adenocarcinoma cell line) that expressed BTAA. BTAA by itself is not very immunogenic, so potentially the future may yield an NLP–enhanced BTAA vaccine. It is not known which compounds in NLP are responsible for the activity (Mandal–Ghosh et al. 2007). Survival data of the mice and rats was not reported.

The triterpenoid nimbolide from neem flowers was shown to restrict cancer cell proliferation in cancer cell lines U937 (human leukemic monocyte lymphoma), HL-60 (human promyelocytic leukemia), THP1 (human acute monocytic leukemia), and B16 (mouse melanoma). Nimbolide at varying doses caused cell cycle disruption and significantly damaged DNA profiles. Apoptosis resulted with "remarkable lethality" for 60% of cells at 1.2 micromolar of nimbolide, thus making it potentially useful in anticancer therapy (Roy et al. 2007).

Pregnancy and Contraception

While there are no neem pregnancy and contraception products available in the United States, in India one product is currently in clinical trials. Praneem (licensed to Panacea Biotec, India) is a polyherbal vaginal tablet that has proven to be effective in immobilizing sperm (Joshi et al. 2008; Garg et al. 1994). Other studies also reported that neem has pregnancy and contraceptive properties:

Neem oil has antifertility, anti–implantation, and abortifacient properties. Fraction isolated from neem oil, NIM-76, had spermicidal properties without the abortifacient properties, and was an effective vaginal contraceptive. In vitro, NIM-76 selectively kills all human sperm in less than 20 seconds at a concentration of 25 mg/mL. Because it is selective and does not damage normal cells, NIM-76 is said to be a "highly desirable potential vaginal contraceptive agent" (Sharma et al. 1996). Despite these positive results, it does not appear that any such product is yet available commercially.

In addition, neem and seed extracts administered orally at the beginning of the post–implantation stage resulted in pregnancy termination in rodents and primates, without any permanent effects. The mechanism of action is not fully understood (Talwar et al. 1997).

Skin Disorders

Neem can treat many skin disorders, including scabies and lice.

In a paste combination with Curcuma longa (turmeric), neem was used to treat scabies in 814 people—97% of them were cured within 3 to 15 days of application, and no adverse reactions were observed (Charles and Charles 1992).

Furthermore, a new formulation of neem shampoo (identified as Type AP30) has proven to be "highly effective against all stages of head lice" for 66 children (4 to 15 years old) with significant head lice infestations, even after only 10 minutes of exposure time. The percentages of effectiveness ranged from 86% to 97% after a single application of the shampoo; only a second retreatment was needed for most children to remain lice–free, except for a couple living in squalor conditions and one with very fatty hair. No adverse effects were observed (Abdel–Ghaffar and Semmler 2007).

Dental and Oral Care

Neem also has benefits in dental and oral care by inhibiting bacteria that causes tooth decay.

In preliminary findings, neem inhibited *Streptococcus mutans* (bacterium causing tooth decay) and reversed incipient carious lesions (that is, primary dental caries) (Vanka et al. 2001).

When saliva–conditioned hydroxyapatite (a bone salt that strengthens the matrix of teeth and bone) was pretreated with neem extract (from bark sticks) there was major inhibition in some *Streptococcus colonization* on tooth surfaces (Wolinsky et al. 1996). As mango is also known to inhibit other microorganisms that cause dental caries (*Streptococcus mutans*, *Streptococcus salivarius*, *Streptococcus mitis*, and *Streptococcus sanguis*), chewing both mango and neem tree sticks would provide even further benefit (Prashant et al. 2007).

In addition, a neem–extract dental gel significantly reduced plaque and bacteria (*Streptococcus mutans* and *Lactobacilli species* were tested) over the control group that used commercially available mouthwash containing the germicide chlorhexidine gluconate (0.2% w/v) (Pai et al. 2004).

HIV/AIDS

In HIV/AIDS patients, a 12–week oral administration of acetone–water neem leaf extract (IRAB) had a "significant" influence *in vivo* on CD4 cells (which HIV reduces) without any adverse effects in the patients. Of the 60 patients who completed treatment, 50 were completely laboratory–test compliant. The mean levels of CD4 cells increased by 159% in 50 patients, which is a major increase; the number of HIV/AIDS pathologies decreased from the 120 baseline to 5; and significant increases were experienced in body weight (12%), hemoglobin concentration (24%), and lymphocyte differential count (24%). IRAB is recommended as part of an HIV/AIDS drug treatment program (Mbah et al. 2007).

Diabetes

Neem reduced diabetic symptoms in non–insulin dependent diabetics. Ninety participants in three groups were given tulsi (*Ocimum sanctum*), neem leaf powder, or a tulsi–neem leaf powder mixture. Diabetic symptoms were significantly reduced in all groups—commonly polydypsia (excessive thirst), polyuria (increased frequency of urination), polyphagia (excessive hunger) and fatigue, and less commonly sweating, burning feet, itching, and headaches.

As shown in Table 4-2, tulsi alone provided the most significant reduction only for itching. Neem provided the most relief for polyuria, sweating, and burning feet. The tulsi–neem combination provided the most relief for polydypsia, polyphagia, fatigue, and headaches (Kochhar, et al. 2009):

Table 4-2: Reduction of Diabetic Symptoms

Symptom	Group 1 Tulsi	Groups 2 Neem	Group 3 Tulsi– Neem	Highest %
Polyuria	19%	32%	27%	Neem
Sweating	33%	40%	20%	Neem
Burning feet	43%	44%	29%	Neem
Itching	20%	16%	17%	Tulsi
Polydypsia	35%	33%	40%	Tulsi–Neem
Polyphagia	21%	35%	40%	Tulsi–Neem
Fatigue	13%	18%	25%	Tulsi–Neem
Headaches	27%	38%	40%	Tulsi–Neem

Overall, while the tulsi–neem mixture provided the most relief for diabetic symptoms, neem alone was also very effective. It was recommended that tulsi and neem leaves be ingested by diabetic patients to reduce symptoms (Kochhar, et al. 2009).

Antioxidant

Extracts from young flowers and leaves have strong antioxidant potential. An indicator of oxidative stress, malondialdehyde (MDA), was reduced by 46.0% and 50.6% for flower– and leaf–based extracts, respectively, prompting the recommendation to use neem as a vegetable bitter tonic to promote good health (Sithisarn et al. 2005).

Ulcers

Neem bark extract reduced human gastric acid hypersecretion, and gastroesophageal and gastroduodenal ulcers. After 10 weeks, the duodenal ulcers were nearly fully healed; after 6 weeks one case of esophageal ulcer and gastric ulcer were fully healed (Bandyopadhyay et al. 2004).

Safety and Toxicity

Mitchell Fleisher, MD, DHt. DABFM, a double board-certified, homeopathic family physician and executive director of wellness of How2Connect.com, said he has treated hundreds of patients with purified neem extracts. In relation to the safety of neem, he said: "I have not observed a single, serious adverse reaction. Neem is clearly one of the safest—as well as most cost-effective—herbal medicines available today" (Sperber; Fleisher 2012).

The Neem Foundation also reports that neem does not have any negative health effects for humans because it is gentle. In fact, neem has been found to be less toxic than table salt and aspirin in LD50 studies. Where a 58 kg human only needed to ingest .1 L of aspirin and .2 L of table salt to reach that lethal dosage, those same test subjects would need to ingest .45 L of neem (Sperber).

Despite the well–documented safety of neem, as with any bioactive compound, azadirachtin still needs to be treated with care. In a case involving a woman who overdosed on 1 L of neem leaf extract, she became ill with ventricular fibrillation and cardiac arrest. Even at this excessive quantity—a typical recommended dose is a few drops at a time—she recovered within a week in the hospital (Barceloux 2008).

As with any medicine, special care must be taken regarding children. In poisonings of children who died after ingesting the neem seed extract margosa oil, post–mortem autopsies showed swelling of hepatocytes, fatty metamorphosis of liver, depletion of glycogen, mitochondrial pyknosis (cell degeneration), more peroxisomes, and significantly more smooth endoplasmic reticulum (indicating increased detoxification activity) (Barceloux 2008). Detailed information about these poisonings was not available.

Margosa oil has also been shown to cause toxic encephalopathy, especially in infants and young children. The symptoms of poisoning are vomiting, drowsiness, tachypnea (abnormally fast breathing), recurrent generalized seizures (that may lead to coma or cardio–pulmonary arrest (Barceloux 2008)), leucocytosis, and metabolic acidosis. Treatment is primarily supportive and directed toward controlling convulsions. Fatalities and neurological deficits occur but are not common (Lai et al. 1990).

Neem oil is not approved by the Federal Drug Administration for internal human use, but an estimated safe daily dose of azadirachtin is 15 mg/kg body weight (Barceloux 2008).

Neem as Medicine in the Future

Despite the plethora of evidence—both traditional for thousands of years and formally researched—neem products have not been approved for internal use as medicine in the United States.

It is doubtful this lack of approval is solely related to safety nor efficacy of neem as a medicinal agent. Rather, this problem is likely reflective of the barriers in approving natural products in general through the Federal Drug Administration. This issue is discussed in further detail in "Barriers for Neem" on page 33.

Barriers for Neem 5

Despite the credibility of neem among its prominent supporters and its outstanding 2,000–year track record, there are several barriers in the way of getting neem into the supermarket in a wide–scale manner.

Medicinal Agent Issues

Neem has been a reliable medicinal agent in traditional medicine for centuries—that has not been challenged.

Despite a plethora of health products on the Internet including neem oil promoted as both a female and male contraceptive (Neem Products), neem–based products have not reached the consumer shelves in the United States for any internal medicinal applications.

Unlike the modes of action for pesticide applications, the modes of action for neem chemicals in human medicinal applications are unfortunately not as well understood nor described in published studies. Sadly, this fact contributes to the difficulty in approving neem as a medicinal product.

Pesticide Product Issues

Even after several pesticide products on the U.S. market, neem from natural sources has failed to be used as a good lead in the production of synthetic insecticides (Ishaaya, et al. 2007).

General Barriers

In the past, the barriers to neem becoming produced widespread commercially included limited supply of the natural resource, standardization and quality control (neem kernels without known azadirachtin content, absence of standardization for formulated products), and registration issues (regulatory approval for the compound mixtures in neem extracts and cost) (Isman, 1997).

Difficulty in Comparing

To further illustrate this point, because of the varying extraction processes, formulation solvents, and formulation adjuvants, comparing neem–based insecticides is "difficult, if not impossible" (Hall and Menn 1999).

In 1993, the government of India created a registration process for neem–based insecticides to correct quality issues, such as differences in oil quality. The products were registered based on the azadirachtin content. In addition, acute toxicity and chemical testing were required for all products. As a result of India's efforts, there is an increasing number of companies registering neem insecticides in many parts of the world (Hall and Menn 1999).

Formulation Issues

Even with standardized oil content, effective formulations are complex to develop, partly because of the "temperamental" nature of the insect targeting, meaning that the efficacy of neem varies even among basic species of mosquitoes. When other natural compounds in combination with neem compounds have boosted the insecticide efficacy significantly, it would conceivably be problematic to formulate an insecticide that knowingly does otherwise.

Chemical Properties Issues

The water solubility of azadirachtin is negligible, at 50 ug/mL, has been a limiting factor in its use as a biopesticide or in herbal medicine. Boosting formulations with such compounds as cyclodextrins increases the water solubility of azadirachtin, from a range of 1.3 to 3.5 mg/mL, depending on the cyclodextrin, and show promise as indicated through related patents (Liu et al. 2005). Strategies such as these are useful in future formulations.

In addition, since azadirachtin biodegrades quickly by sunlight (Capinera 2008), training and education would need to be a component of the integrated management approach to pests so that users know the best method and timing of applications.

Patent Issues

And, not uncommon to new applications of bio products, there are patent issues. There is said to be over 90 patents issued worldwide (Benny 2005) to companies for inventions of products from neem. Traditional users of neem claim that some of these patents are invalid—they have been known in traditional medicine for 2,000 years (Cseke, et al. 2006).

In 2000, the European Patent Office revoked a patent from USDA and W.R. Grace for a neem tree fungicide, citing that it was already in use in India in a traditional way (Benny 2005).

Regulatory Issues

The relatively low market share of botanical pesticides versus the multimillion dollar regulatory costs causes an insurmountable hurdle for many botanical pesticides to reach the commercial market. In the United States, registering a new active ingredient can start at more than $250,000 and possibly exceed $2 million.

Moreover, botanicals tend to be complex mixtures (unlike synthetic chemicals), making the registration process even more difficult. Supporters of botanical pesticides suggest that the registration requirement needs to be modified for environmentally safe botanical pesticides (Isman, 1997).

Yet another hurdle is the waned interest in natural insecticides compared to genetically modified plants (Rai and Carpinella 2006).

Conclusion

The place of neem in traditional medicine has been established for centuries. Despite this impressive history, it has many hurdles yet to overcome to gain widespread acceptance in Western society for its medicinal applications. Neem is the wonder tree it is purported to be, and markers point in a positive direction for its future in terms of proven applications and increased acceptance by the scientific community.

Bibliography

Abdel–Ghaffar F, Semmler M. Efficacy of neem seed extract shampoo on head lice of naturally infected humans in Egypt. Parasitol Res. 2007, 100(2):329–32.

Anuradha A, Annadurai RS. Biochemical and molecular evidence of azadirachtin binding to insect actins. Current Science 2008, 95(11).

Azadirachta indica. AgroForestryTree Database website. http://www.worldagroforestrycentre.org.

Bandyopadhyay U, Biswas K, Sengupta A, Moitra P, Dutta P, Sarkar D, Debnath P, Ganguly CK, Banerjee RK. Clinical studies on the effect of Neem (Azadirachta indica) bark extract on gastric secretion and gastroduodenal ulcer. Life Sci. 2004, 75:2867–2878.

Barceloux, D. Medical Toxicology of Natural Substances. John Wiley & Sons, Inc. 2008.

Benny J. Environmental Studies. Tata McGraw–Hill. 2005.

Boeke SJ, Boersma MG, Alink GM, van Loon JJ, van Huis A, Dicke M, Rietjens IM. Safety evaluation of Neem (Azadirachta indica) derived pesticides. J Ethnopharmacol. 2004, 94(1):25–41.

Bose A, Haque E, Baral R. Neem leaf preparation induces apoptosis of tumor cells by releasing cytotoxic cytokines from human peripheral blood mononuclear cells. Phytother Res. 2007, 21(10):914–20.

Brandt GE, Schmidt MD, Prisinzano TE, Blagg BS. Gedunin, a novel Hsp90 inhibitor: semisynthesis of derivatives and preliminary structure–activity relationships. J Med Chem. 2008, 51(20):6495–502.

Capinera J. Encyclopedia of Entomology. Springer Science+Business Media B.V. 2008.

Carreira E, Kvaerno L. Classics in Stereoselective Synthesis. Wiley–VCH Verlag GmbH & Co. 2009.

Charles V, Charles SX. The use and efficacy of Azadirachta indica ADR (neem) and Curcuma longa (turmeric) in scabies. A pilot study. Trop Geogr Med. 1992, 44(1–2):178–81.

Collinge DB, Munk L, Cooke BM. Sustainable disease management in a European context. Eur J Plant Pathol. 2008, 121:213–216.

Cseke LJ, Kirakosyan A, Kaufman PB, Warber SL, Duke J, Brielmann HL. Natural Products from Plants, 2nd edition. Taylor & Francis Group. 2006.

Department of Forest Resources and Agrifoods, Newfoundland Forestry Service. The 2002 Proposed Forest Protection Program Against the Balsam Fir Sawfly Using Aerially Applied Botanical Insecticide Neemix® 4.5 (Azadirachtin). 2002.

Devakumar C, Kumar R. Total synthesis of azadirachtin: A chemical odyssey. Current Science. 2008, 95(5).

Dewick PM. Medicinal Natural Products. John Wiley & Sons, Ltd. 2001.

Dhingra S, Walia S, Kumar J, Singh S, Singh G, Parmar BS. Field efficacy of azadirachtin-A, tetrahydroazadirachtin-A, NeemAzal and endosulfan against key pests of okra (Abelmoschus esculentus). Pest Manag Sci. 2008, 64(11):1187–94.

Environmental Protection Agency website. Label Review Manual.

Fleisher, Mitchell, MD, DHt., DABFM, DcABCT. Email correspondence. January 21, 2012.

Free Patents Online website. http://www.freepatentsonline.com.

Garg S, Doncel G, Chabra S, Upadhyay SN, Talwar GP. Synergistic spermicidal activity of Neem seed extract, reetha saponins and quinine hydrochloride. Contraception. 1994, 50(2):185–90.

Gianotti RL, Bomblies A, Dafalla M, Issa–Arzika I, Duchemin JB, Eltahir EA. Efficacy of local neem extracts for sustainable malaria vector control in an African village. Malar J. 2008 7:138.

Gokhale SB, Kokate CK, Purohit AP. A Text Book of Pharmacognosy. Nirali Prakashan. 2009.

Gunasekaran K, Reddy CMR. Laboratory evaluation of NeemAzal T/S 1% EC for its larvicidal and insect growth regulating activity against three vector species, Anopheles stephensi, Culex quinquefasciatus and Aedes aegypti. Annual Report 2003. Vector Control Research Centre. 2003.

Hall FR, Menn JJ, editors. Biopesticides Use and Delivery. Humana Press. 1999.

Harikrishnan R, Balasundaram C. In vitro and *in vivo* studies of the use of some medicinal herbals against the pathogen Aeromonas hydrophila in goldfish. J Aquat Anim Health. 2008, 20(3):165–76.

Hoque M, Bari ML, Inatsu Y, Juneja VK, Kawamoto S. Antibacterial activity of guava (Psidium guajava L.) and neem (Azadirachta indica A. Juss.) extracts against foodborne pathogens and spoilage bacteria. Foodborne Pathog Dis. 2007, 4(4):481–8.

Infinity Pharmaceuticals website. http://www.infi.com.

Ishaaya I, Nauen R, Horowitz AR, editors. Insecticides Design Using Advanced Technologies. Springer–Verlag. 2007.

Isman MB. Neem and other botanical insecticides: barriers to commercialization. Phytoparasitica. 1997, 25(4):339–344.

Isman M. Neem insecticides. Pesticide Outlook. October 1997.

Johnson S, Morgan D, Peiris C. Development of the major triterpenoids and oil in the fruit and seeds of neem (Azadirachta indica). Annals of Botany. 1996, 78: 383–388.

Joshi SN, Dutta S, Kumar BK, Katti U, Kulkarni S, Risbud A, Mehendale S. Expanded safety study of Praneem polyherbal vaginal tablet among HIV–uninfected women in Pune, India: a phase II clinical trial report. Sexually Transmitted Infections. 2008, 84:343–347.

Kochhar A, Sharma N, Sachdeva R. Effect of supplementation of tulsi (Ocimum sanctum) and neem (Azadirachta indica) leaf powder on diabetic symptoms, anthropometric parameters and blood pressure of non insulin dependent male diabetics. Ethno–Med. 2009, 3(1): 5–9.

Koul O, Wahab S, editors. Neem: Today and in the New Millenium. Kluwer Academic Publishers. 2004.

Kraiss H, Cullen EM. Insect growth regulator effects of azadirachtin and neem oil on survivorship, development and fecundity of Aphis glycines (Homoptera: Aphididae) and its predator, Harmonia axyridis (Coleoptera: Coccinellidae). Pest Manag Sci. 2008, 64(6):660–8.

Kumar S, Suresh PK, Vijayababu MR, Arunkumar A, Arunakaran J. Anticancer effects of ethanolic neem leaf extract on prostate cancer cell line (PC–3). J Ethnopharmacol. 2006, 105(1–2):246–50.

Lai SM, Lim KW, Cheng HK. Margosa oil poisoning as a cause of toxic encephalopathy. Singapore Med J. 1990, 31(5):463–5.

Liu Y, Chen G, Chena Y, Linb J. Inclusion complexes of azadirachtin with native and methylated cyclodextrins: solubilization and binding ability. Bioorganic & Medicinal Chemistry. 2005, 13:4037–4042.

Mandal–Ghosh I, Chattopadhyay U, Baral R. Neem leaf preparation enhances Th1 type immune response and anti–tumor immunity against breast tumor associated antigen. Cancer Immun. 2007, 7:8.

Mbah AU, Udeinya IJ, Shu EN, Chijioke CP, Nubila T, Udeinya F, Muobuike A, Mmuobieri A, Obioma MS. Fractionated neem leaf extract is safe and increases CD4+ cell levels in HIV/AIDS patients. Am J Ther. 2007, 14(4):369–74.

Mordue (Luntz) JA, Nisbet A. Azadirachtin from the neem tree Azadirachta indica: its action against insects. An. Soc. Entomol. Brasil. 2000, 29(4): 615–632.

Morovati M, Mahmoudi M, Ghazi–Khansari M, Khalil Aria A, Jabbari L. Sterility and abortive effects of the commercial neem (Azadirachta indica A. Juss.) extract NeemAzal– T/S® on female rat (Rattus norvegicus). Turk J Zool. 2008, 32:155–162.

Muñoz–Valenzuela S, Ibarra–López AA, Rubio–Silva LM, Valdez–Dávila H, Borboa–Flores J. Neem tree morphology and oil content. Issues in new crops and new uses. ASHS Press. 2007.

Neem Foundation website. http://www.Neemfoundation.org.

Neem Products website. http://www.neemproducts.com.

Pai MR, Acharya LD, Udupa N. Evaluation of antiplaque activity of Azadirachta indica leaf extract gel—a 6–week clinical study. J Ethnopharmacol. 2004, 90(1):99–103.

Peshin R, Dhawan AK, editors. Integrated Pest Management: Innovation–Development Process. Springer Science+Business Media B.V. 2009.

Prashant GM, Chandu GN, Murulikrishna KS, Shafiulla MD. The effect of mango and neem extract on four organisms causing dental caries: Streptococcus mutans, Streptococcus salivavius, Streptococcus mitis, and Streptococcus sanguis: an in vitro study. Indian J Dent Res. 2007, 18(4):148–51.

Rai M, Carpinella MC. Advances in Phytomedicine. Elsevier. 2006.

Reutemann P, Ehrlich A. Neem oil: an herbal therapy for alopecia causes dermatitis. Dermatitis. 2008, 19(3):E12–5.

Roy MK, Kobori M, Takenaka M, Nakahara K, Shinmoto H, Isobe S, Tsushida T. Antiproliferative effect on human cancer cell lines after treatment with nimbolide extracted from an edible part of the neem tree (Azadirachta indica). Phytother Res. 2007, 21(3):245–50.

Roy MK, Kobori M, Takenaka M, Nakahara K, Shinmoto H, Tsushida T. Inhibition of colon cancer (HT-29) cell proliferation by a triterpenoid isolated from Azadirachta indica is accompanied by cell cycle arrest and up–regulation of p21. Planta Med. 2006, 72(10):917–23.

Schoonhoven LM, van Loon JJA, Dicke M. Insect–Plant Biology. Oxford University Press. 2005.

Shanmugasundaram R, Jeyalakshmi T, Dutt MS, Murthy PB. Larvicidal activity of neem and karanja oil cakes against mosquito vectors, Culex quinquefasciatus (say), Aedes aegypti (L.) and Anopheles stephensi (L.). J Environ Biol. 2008, 29(1):43–5.

Sharma SK, SaiRam M, Ilavazhagan G, Devendra K, Shivaji SS, Selvamurthy W. Mechanism of action of NIM-76: a novel vaginal contraceptive from neem oil. Contraception. 1996, 54(6):373–8.

Singh A, Singh DK. Molluscicidal activity of Lawsonia inermis and its binary and tertiary combinations with other plant derived molluscicides. Indian J Exp Biol. 2001, 39(3):263–8.

Sithisarn P, Supabphol R, Gritsanapan W. Antioxidant activity of Siamese neem tree (VP1209). J Ethnopharmacol. 2005, 99(1):109–12.

Sperber Haas, Sheila, editor. Neem: A hands-on guide to one of the world's most versatile herbs.

Subapriya R, Nagini S. Medicinal properties of neem leaves: a review. Curr Med Chem Anticancer Agents. 2005, 5(2):149–6.

Talwar GP, Raghuvanshi P, Misra R, Mukherjee S, Shah S. Plant immunomodulators for termination of unwanted pregnancy and for contraception and reproductive health. Immunol Cell Biol. 1997, 75(2):190–2.

University of Delaware website. Pesticide Safety. http://ag.udel.edu.

Vanka A, Tandon S, Rao SR, Udupa N, Ramkumar P. The effect of indigenous neem Azadirachta indica mouth wash on Streptococcus mutans and lactobacilli growth. Indian J Dent Res. 2001, 12(3):133–44.

Vatandoost H, Hanafi–Bojd AA. Laboratory evaluation of 3 repellents against Anopheles stephensi in the Islamic Republic of Iran. East Mediterr Health J. 2008, 14(2):260–7.

Veitch, GE, Beckmann E, Burke BJ, Boyer A, Maslen SL, Ley SV. Synthesis of azadirachtin: a long but successful journey. Angew. Chem. Int. Ed. 2007, 46:7629 –7632.

Watson RR, Preedy VR. Botanical Medicine in Clinical Practice. CAB International. 2008.

Wolinsky LE, Mania S, Nachnani S, Ling S. The inhibiting effect of aqueous Azadirachta indica (Neem) extract upon bacterial properties influencing in vitro plaque formation. J Dent Res. 1996, 75(2):816–22.

Bibliography

About the Author

Pamela Paterson is an author, consultant, college instructor, and speaker. She has written hundreds of articles, papers, and books in over 30 subject areas. She has a bachelor's degree in journalism and a master's degree in science from the University of Maryland.

Pamela was inducted into academic honor society Phi Kappa Phi, joining notable members Linus C. Pauling, Hilary Rodham Clinton, and Jimmy Carter.

Global companies such as Hewlett-Packard, Siemens, and Honda have sought her writing services, which she has expanded to meet the needs of individuals and small businesses. Pamela may be contacted at pamthewriter@gmail.com.

Index

Index

Made in the USA
Middletown, DE
16 January 2015